Contact us at: getrichpromotingparties@gmail.com

Published by:

Energy is Everything Publishing LLC
Las Vegas, NV 89147
ISBN 978-1-7379176-1-8 (paperback)
ISBN 978-1-7379176-0-1 (ebook)
www.getrichpromotingparitesandconcerts.com[1]

Table of Contents

INTRODUCTION

We want to thank you for your trust and for allowing us to guide you on your journey to building a successful promotions business. Your level of success and the amount of money you can make in your endeavors will depend on how motivated and ambitious you are. In our own experience, we have made as much as six figures throwing just one party! For a weekly hip-hop event at a popular nightclub, when properly promoted using the information we will be providing to you in this book, the revenue after expenses was over $20,000 weekly. In this business, you could make millions!

We have outlined step-by-step instructions to help you build an event and promotions empire. We will provide instructions, examples, and common tools we use to help you on your way, and describe common mistakes to avoid that could derail your efforts. Always remember that any road to success is bumpy and you will face many challenges. With this guide, you will have the advantage of learning from two people with over 30 years of combined experience in the promotions business for events and parties. We have experience with all types of event planning and promotions, ranging from concerts and charity events to teen nights, fashion shows, nightclub parties, political events, and more!

Many people might think that it's easy to put together and organize an event or party, and the truth is that it actually is, but only once you know the proper formula. In this book, my business partner and I will show you not only the proper formulas, but the solutions as well.

As you read this book, you will see that we have also included worksheets for you to complete that will help you through the processes. These worksheets are extremely important as you begin building your business. Over time, you won't need the worksheets anymore as you will have learned how to run through the necessary tasks in your own mind.

Now, please allow us to introduce ourselves and our backgrounds.

ABOUT THE AUTHORS

G.M. Caraballo

My name is G.M. Caraballo, and I've been in this business for well over 20 years. I have seen the bottom as well as the top in this industry. As I've gotten a little older, I've wanted to share my experiences to teach people the correct way to promote and organize events.

I grew up in a not-so-great neighborhood in one of the most economically disadvantaged cities in the northern United States. At a young age, I got involved in many illegal things as a way to make money. After knowing what it was like to have money and living a certain lifestyle, there was no way I could ever go back to living "without" again. After a hard bump in the road that took years of my freedom away, one of my best friends asked me to switch my profession and get into promoting events. My friend was a very well-known radio host, event promoter, and even had his own TV show.

At the time, I had just gotten out of prison and I was right back to what I knew best - "Gettin' Money!" - and not the legal way. My friend and I grew up together in the northern U.S., and he was worried that I was going to either end up dead or back in prison. He invited me down to Miami to visit him, and when I saw how he was living, I told myself that I had to switch my profession. My friend was living like a super star and making money the legal way.

After that trip to Miami, I got into promoting events. To be honest with you, I lost a lot of money on my first few parties and events, but only because I thought I knew everything and did not listen to my friend's advice. After several failed parties, I picked myself up and asked my friend for his help. I flew him up and he showed me the ropes of the event promotions business. Learning directly from his experiences, I became very successful and made a lot of money. After being in the business for a long time. I even started coming up with my own strategies to boost my business and make even more cash.

Organizing and promoting events has opened so many doors for me, including owning several major nightclubs and bars. If you are ready to change your life, or have always been interested in learning how to promote and organize events, then this is the book for you. Absorb as much information as you can from our years of experience, and good luck on your journey into the world of nightlife marketing and promotions.

- G.M Caraballo

J.R. Magyar

My name is J.R. Magyar, and I started working in nightclubs at the age of 18. I worked as a security guy for about three nights before I started working in the VIP area of the venue. I learned a tremendous amount regarding customer service, VIP reservation, client relations, client management, and the pivotal role VIP sales play in a venue's overall success.

I opened several venues as a VIP director in multiple cities in Florida. I've worked as a Door Manager at venues during huge holiday parties with tons of other promoters. I've learned all the tricks that the venue staff used to steal and scam, so I can now teach you how NOT to be taken advantage of by venue staff during these parties. This information will be key to your success.

I remember one party for Memorial Day weekend where the promoters increased the cover charge by $10 every half hour. As the Door Manager for the venue, I was stationed just outside in the parking lot with two door guys checking IDs and two cashier girls.

The five of us were left on our own, so no promoters or their employees were with us. As the night went on, the cover charge had risen to $60 per person. I had several large groups of 7-10 people trying to get into the venue, but they didn't want to pay up to $600 in cover charges for their groups. So, I would tell them to pay $450 for the group. I would then pocket the cash, tell the cashiers not to ring them in, and let the group walk right into the venue. By the end of the night, each of the five of us walked away with almost $500 in cash. We stole $2,500 in cover charges from the promoters and all because they didn't have an employee or door person watching the main entrance and collecting the cash for the cover charge.

I have also managed very large VIP sections, some of which had up to 75 VIP tables on 3 floors with 8-10 waitresses per night. I worked with multiple promoters to book VIP reservations, track sales, calculate and distribute payouts, and maintained relationships between the promoters and owners. I've handed out flyers, made parking lot runs, mingled at business parties, and have promoted not only the Venues I was working for, but myself and the promoters themselves as well. I've seen a very popular venue go bankrupt because even as the promoters packed the venue for months on end, the owner thought he could be greedy and steal from his own staff and the promoters. One by one, the promoters quit, and the venue and its owner got such a bad rap that it shut down within six months.

So even if you build a great promotional business, you will inevitably run into scumbag owners, but there are many fair, honest, and loyal owners out there as well. Always be on your toes, use the advice from this book, and you will be a step, or two ahead of the competition.

- J.R. Magyar

So now that you know a little about us, our backgrounds, and our experience in this industry, let's take the first step together and welcome you to "Get Rich Promoting Parties & Concerts."

PART I

When choosing the type of event or party, there are a few key factors to consider. We will cover each of these throughout this book along with some true stories that detail some of the challenges we have faced. This is one of the most important steps in organizing your event or party. You will need to be VERY honest with yourself regarding your budget, clientele, commitment, personal preferences, and your desire for success. Your first challenge will be to decide whether you want to start your business by having various one-time events, like concerts, graduation parties, birthday parties, holiday parties, and/or special events, or if you want to build a weekly, long-term event or recurring party at a new or existing venue. This is key since you will have different budgets, promotions, and talent for a single event versus a weekly party.

One-Time Event vs Weekly Events

A great way to help you decide what path may be best for you is to start with something small like a birthday, bachelor/bachelorette, or graduation party. These types of events are great starting points since many of the steps in this book just have to be scaled up for larger or weekly parties. You are also usually inviting or dealing with friends and family with these types of parties. They are more likely to participate in your event, and it's a great confidence booster.

We are going to describe a birthday party scenario. This is an example of a one time event that is an easy way for you to get into this business. How you negotiate and interact with the owner will set up your business for future success. We will show you how to negotiate with the owner, whether you choose to do one-time events or want to promote a weekly one.

BIRTHDAY PARTY BASICS

- 100 people have been invited

- Good weather is expected
- Venue hours are 10 PM - 2 AM, and it holds up to 350 people
- There is ample parking near the venue for guests
- The party is being held on a Thursday night since the venue t Typically only expects between 50-100 people that night
- DJ will play Top 40/Hip Hop and take requests
- You will supply a small amount of decorations
- Venue has a 2-for-1 drink special and no cover charge

Using the listed event criteria, here's how we would suggest you negotiate various elements of your party with the venue owner or manager.

First and foremost, you will have to make an appointment to meet with the owner or manager. Ideally, you will want to meet in person, at the venue, to begin building a good business relationship. Be polite and professional when setting up the time to meet. Let them know that you are planning a very special birthday party with 50-100 people and that you would like to discuss some party details at the venue.

If the owner or manager is interested, they will ask a few more questions and then have no problem meeting with you at some point prior to the event. If the owner or manager is reluctant to meet up with you, that will raise some red flags for us. In this case, you should probably look for a different venue to have your party at.

Having an interested owner or manager for a reasonably large birthday party or event is ideally what you are looking for. This shows that they are open to all new business opportunities and relationships. These types of owners or managers will help you build your business.

Be Prepared

D o your homework regarding the venue; its popular nights, it's typical crowds, various drink specials, and past events that have been held there. We will discuss in greater detail how to choose the best venue for your events in a later chapter.

Prepare an Event Proposal

Prepare an event proposal for the owner or manager. Your proposal should include the following:

- Type of Event: Birthday, Graduation, Bachelor/Bachelorette, etc.
- Expected number of Guests: 50-100
- Music Type:
- Time of Event:
- Dress Code: (Be sure to get the venue's approval if you plan on doing a themed party or if it's outside the typical code.)

Explain why you are doing this event. How do you plan on marketing and promoting the event? Discuss any items that you might want to bring for the event:

- Birthday Cake
- Decorations
- Balloons
- Special Entertainment
- Other Items

Depending on the complexity of the event, the proposal could be quite long. You want to do your best to keep it short and sweet. Get to the point and use a bullet-point format as shown above to make it easy to read for the owner or manager.

There are also sample worksheets throughout the book that you can modify for your own events and parties, and here is an example of a birthday party proposal:

EVENT/PARTY PROPOSAL
Birthday Party

We are looking to celebrate a Birthday Party at your venue on Thursday night, (DATE). This party is for a close friend of ours, and we are looking to invite over 100 friends and family members.

We would like an area set aside for our group that we may utilize from about 10 PM - 2 AM. Any type of music is fine and we were hoping the DJ might be able to do some shout outs or play certain requested songs.

If you could provide some small decorations in our area, a drink or bottle special, no cover charge, and a space in a cooler for a large birthday cake, that would be appreciated. All of the guests will be dressed according to the venue's dress code.

We would also like to be able to do the following:

- have sparklers
- champagne toast at midnight
- balloons

Your help in celebrating our friend's special birthday is appreciated.

The Meeting

- Make sure you introduce yourself. "Hi Mr./Ms. (Owner's Name), my name is J.R., and thank you for taking the time to meet with me. The reason I am here is ..."
- Always shake the owner/manager's hand, make and maintain good eye contact and be professional. The way you dress will give the owner/manager and indication of what type of crowd you might be bringing to their venue.

- BE ON TIME OR EARLY to all of your appointments. There is an old saying, "If you aren't 15 minutes early, you are already late." Punctuality and professionalism will help to establish your credibility in this industry.

Since you are discussing having a one-time event with the owner/manager, your focus should be on presenting how your event will add value to the owner/manager and the venue. Review the event proposal with them, and discuss why you're having the event, why you have chosen THIS venue, the number of people you are expecting, and if you have any VIP reservations or bottle requests from your guest list. Additionally, if your guests like certain types of drinks or bottles, you can discuss possible drink or bottle specials with the owner/manager.

Be attentive and listen for feedback from the owner/manager. The typical venue will be very receptive to an extra 50-100 people on a typically slower night. Once you have a positive reaction from the owner/manager regarding your event and an agreement to host your party, you can then discuss potential future events at that point.

Here are a few simple examples of how to pitch your business to the owner/manager:

《 》

OPTION A

"THANK YOU, MR./MS., (owner/manager) for this opportunity to host this event at your venue. This is a new business that I am starting. I'm hoping that by making this event a success, there might be opportunities to collaborate on future parties/events."

Wait for the manager/owner's response. They will typically be open to this suggestion but might want to see the results of a few successful events or parties first.

OPTION B

"Thank you, Mr./Ms., (owner/manager) for the opportunity to host this event at your venue. I'm looking to promote a new night at your venue weekly. I would like to use this event· to prove to you that I can bring a good crowd to your venue that will benefit both of us. Wait for the owner/manager to respond. Most likely, they will agree to have that discussion after the party.

These two options are simple suggestions that you can tailor to your personality. Your network of friends will always have a birthday, graduation or bachelor/bachelorette party coming up. You can use these types of events and parties to assess your comfort level throwing one-time parties versus establishing a weekly event. Having confidence in this business is extremely important. If your budget is smaller, doing one-time events can be a better fit. They allow you to boost your confidence, credibility, and cash flow. If you have extra cash, you are in a better position to start a weekly event with a venue. Abide by your word and honor your commitments with the owner/manager and also any vendors, sponsors, or partners.

Before any planning can be done, you must first decide upon a realistic budget for your event or party. Be responsible and reasonable with your extra cash. Remember that you are building a business. We do not recommend spending all of your business cash on your first event. If you are starting with a one-time event, your budget could be up to $2,500. If you are doing a large concert or event, you could potentially spend up to $50,000 or more on talent, equipment, promotions, and staffing.

Included next is an example of an Expense Sheet for you to review. Blank sheets are also provided for your use. Anytime you are planning events or parties, USE THESE SHEETS. They will help you realize what you can or can't financially do. Also, after any event or party, you want to add up ALL of your expenses and profits to see how much you made from that particular event or party.

《 》

EVENT: SAMPLE EVENT
OPENING DATE: / /

VENUE:
ADDRESS:

EXPENSES (WITH EXPLANATIONS)
BUDGET AVAILABLE: $ 2000
NOTES:

EXPENDITURES:

1) VENUE: For security, off-duty police, and staff provided by the venue.
2) FLYERS/POSTERS: Avg. rate of return is 5%. If you hand out 1,000 flyers, expect around 50 people.
3) STREET TEAM: Avg. about $12-15/hr per person, plus gas & food or what you negotiate.
4) RADIO: Varies depending on your city and the time slots available for your ads and their length.
5) TV: Similar considerations to radio.
6) DJ/TALENT/RIDER: Varies depending on artists or performers, time of year, and special requests.
7) CASHIER/VIP CASHIER1:1. Avg. cost is $75-100 per shift.
8) GRAPHICS DESIGN: Typically $100-$350 for a basic flyer design and artwork for the party.
9) SOCIAL MEDIA: Ads & Influencers. This is based on the costs of the ads & negotiations with influencers
10) SECURITY: Avg. $75-100 per shift.

11) WRISTBANDS: Sometimes provided by the venue, but you may want to use your own to reduce theft or issues with door staff
12) DECORATIONS: Depends on the type of party

13) GIVEAWAYS: Raffles of gift cards, bottles, or other items to the first 50-100 people.
14) EQUIPMENT RENTALS: Includes things like sound equipment, smoke machines, lighting foam, etc.
15) PERMITS & LICENSES: Depends on the type of party, where, and the time, esp. outdoor events or street parties.
16) MERCHANDISE: Items like t-shirts, hats, wristbands, or other items to boost sales.
17) MISCELLANEOUS Unexpected potential costs like costumes, dancers, beverages, extra staff, cancellation fees, etc.

BUDGET: $
TOTAL EXPENSES: -
OVER/UNDER BUDGET: $

INCOMES

1) COVER CHARGE: $
2) BAR SPLIT:
3) SPONSORSHIPS:
4) MERCHANDISE:
5) TICKET SALES:
6) MISCELLANEOUS: +

TOTAL INCOME: $

TOTAL INCOME: $
TOTAL EXPENSES: -

TOTAL PROFIT: $

EVENT: _____

VENUE: _____

ADDRESS: _____

EXPENSES

BUDGET AVAILABLE: $ _____

NOTES _____

_____

_____

_____

EXPENDITURES:

1) VENUE: _____

2) FLYERS/POSTERS _____

3) STREET TEAM: _____

4) RADIO _____

5) TV: _____

6) DJ/TALENT/RIDER: _____

7) CASHIER/VIP CASHIER _____

8) GRAPHICS DESIGN: _____

9) SOCIAL MEDIA: _____

10) SECURITY: _____

_____

_____

11) WRISTBANDS: _____

12) DECORATIONS: _____

13) GIVEAWAYS: _____

14) Equipment RENTALS: _____

15) PERMITS & LICENSES _____

16) MERCHANDISE: _____

17) MISCELLANIOUS: _____

BUDGET: $ _____

TOTAL EXPENSES: - _____

OVER/UNDER BUDGET: $ _____

INCOMES

1) COVER CHARGE: $ _____

2) BAR SPLIT: _____

3) SPONSORSHIPS: _____

4) MERCHANDISE: _____

5) TICKET SALES: _____

6) MISCELLANEOUS: + _____

TOTAL INCOME: $ _____

TOTAL INCOME: $ _____

TOTAL EXPENSES - _____

TOTAL PROFIT: $ _____

CLIENTELE

After establishing your budget, you must seriously and honestly review who your potential clientele currently are or who they might be. Initially, your network of friends and their friends will be the easiest for you to target. If you follow the birthday party example and have a successful small event, you should now have some credibility with those people, their friends, and the venue. This broadens your clientele and customer base. When planning and building your event or party, be mindful that the type of music will be a factor in who might show up. Typically, a Top 40 night will attract a variety of people from all backgrounds. This increases your appealability and widens your potential customer base.

Fair warning: when doing any type of event or party, your friends are usually the ones that expect something for free. This is a conversation that needs to be addressed with your core group of friends. We would recommend explaining that you are starting a new business and their support is greatly appreciated. Explain that the venue controls many aspects of the party and that you can't give them free cover or drinks. You might be able to get them discounts in the future, but this early on, you need to make a good impression with the owner/manager. If they are your real friends, they will show up to support you no matter what. You can also ask your friends to promote your events on their social media pages.

CHOOSING THE THEME FOR YOUR EVENT OR PARTY

After determining who your target market will be and with your budget in mind, you can now choose the theme for your event/party. A theme could be a Top 40 Ladies' Night or a Hip-Hop party. It could be a Salsa night, teen party, or College Night. Doing research for your area is very important. Knowing what types of themed events do best at the venues in your locale will help you decide on what is best for you and your clientele. We discuss this topic throughout the book. Our best advice is to "Go with what you know." If you like Hip-Hop music, do a Hip-Hop event. If you like Top 40, then start a Top 40 Dance Party. If you like country music, do a country music party. Build an event or party that you would want to go to. Use this sample worksheet to help you decide on what to offer your clientele. We want to know what our competition is offering so that we can match them or beat them with creativity and incentives.

THEME RESEARCH WORKSHEET
(Template)

Night of your Event/Party:
Projected Event/Party Date:

Venue Name: Night Theme:
Drink Specials: Cover Charge:
Bottle Specials: Avg.# of Customers:
Notes:

Venue Name: Night Theme:
Drink Specials: Cover Charge
Bottle Specials   Avg. # of Customers:
Notes:

Venue Name: Night Theme:
Drink Specials: Cover Charge:
Bottle Specials: Avg. # of Customers:
Notes:

Venue Name: Night Theme:
Drink Specials: Cover Charge:
Bottle Specials: Avg.# of Customers:
NotP.s:

Venue Name: Night Theme:
Drink Specials: Cover Charge:
Bottle Specials: Avg.# of Customers
Notes:

STORY: A "NEGATIVE" EXPERIENCE

This is a personal story about an unsuccessful event. It was one of my earliest events, and I'd worked out a deal at a very nice nightclub for a Thursday. The nightclub held about 1,500 people. The price for every Thursday night was $800 because it was a slower night of the week and they were normally closed on Thursday nights.

I ordered a box of 5,000 flyers about two weeks before the event and purchased a $2,000 radio package. I had already worked out a deal to fly in one of my buddy's DJs from Miami at $800, plus the cost of a hotel, the airfare, transportation, and food. I also hired extra staff for the doors and a cashier of my own.

Back then, there was no Facebook, Instagram, or any other social media or internet marketing, so you really had to put the work in.

What I did was put large numbers of flyers in local stores that I shopped at and barber shops. Also, every time I saw people I knew, I would talk to them about the event, invite them, and asked them to pass out some of my flyers to their buddies. I thought I could pack the place because I knew a lot of people and because I had a DJ from another big city, plus I had purchased the radio advertisement package.

The Thursday of the event came around. I went and bought myself a new suit and got a fresh, new haircut because I thought I had to look sharp since it was my event. The doors opened, and as soon as I had arrived and started hanging out with my friends and family, I started drinking. The music was going and I kept getting called to the door. Every time I went, it was somebody I knew with their friends and pointing out they'd brought people as I'd asked them to do, expecting me to let them all in for free. Since I was drinking, having a good time, and I was the one in charge of the door, I was letting the people I knew and their friends in at no charge. I was also spending big money at the bar with other people I knew and their friends.

At the end of the night, it was time for me to close out, count the money, pay the cashiers and the others that were working for me. I was too damn drunk to do any of that, so I told them I would pay them the following morning. The next day, when I woke up, I started to count the money from the night before, and I think there might have been $700 that had been collected at the door. There might have been over 200 people there, but most came in for free because of me. I was my own best customer and did not even realize this at the time. This went on for a few months, and every week, I would be another $6,000 to $7,000 in the red and could not figure out what was going on. Eventually, I realized that I didn't know what the heck I was doing, and I was just continuing to dig myself deeper and deeper into the hole. Finally, I called my friend and flew him in to come show me the ropes. After working with him for a few weeks and doing the things that are in this book, my event turned around and I started making money.

Your first priority is to get established and create a business that works. Once you have everything under control and are making good money, you can hire somebody that you trust to do your closings and pay outs. We strongly recommend that you do not get drunk at your events or parties while you are trying to build your brand.

We have also lost lots of money by not protecting ourselves with fair contracts from artists and certain venues. Some venues will see that you are packing their place, get greedy, and then get rid of you, or demand a bigger percentage of the door charge if you are going to stay there.

We advise you to do your research of the venue and make sure you are doing business with good people. Also, make sure to stand by your word and be responsible for yourself. As a promoter, you have become part of that venue, so be sure to help out as much as you can. You have to treat the place as if it were your own because if you are bringing people in there that will be disrespectful to others, you will be chasing a lot more people out of there and that is your money; money that will not be coming back through those doors.

PART II

CHOOSING THE RIGHT VENUE

Choosing the right venue is an essential component to your event's success. There are several factors that you must consider when selecting the best place to have your party. For us, this is done as we walk through a venue. We have a mental checklist that we utilize to rate each venue that we are considering. We have provided you with a worksheet in this section to help you. You should save every worksheet that you complete for any venue that you walk through or visit. This will help as you plan future events. You can just look back in your files and review all of the worksheets. It is always better to have your first event at a smaller venue. A smaller venue packed, with a line down the street, is actually better for business than having a larger venue that's mostly empty. A packed event creates more buzz and credibility for you, your company, and your parties. We have both had parties at venues that hold 2,000 people or more. For these size venues, you need at least 500 people in the place just to make people feel like it's a good party that they would want to come back to and to tell others about. If you have the ability and network to get 500-1,000 people to show up to your party, then you should choose a venue with a capacity within that same range. This will help in case you don't get the full turn out that you expect and will create a great look for your company and its events.

Your venue can be any place that fits your event's needs and matches your VISION for what your event should be like. Here are a few ideas for you:

- Roller Skating Rinks
- Nightclubs
- Bars

- Concert Venues
- Stadiums
- Outdoor Venue or Parks
- Halls or Auditoriums
- Warehouses
- Restaurants
- Streets in a Neighborhood or a Downtown area
- Strip Clubs
- Breweries
- Hotels
- Docks, Boardwalks, Marinas, Boats, Beaches, or Yachts

As you go through the process of selecting your venue, there are a few topics that we would like to review with you. This information comes from personal experiences that we believe will help you.

VENUE WORKSHEET

Venue: _____   Phone: ( ) _____
ADDRESS: _____ ( ) _____
     _____ WEBSITE: _____

OCCUPANCY: _____ EMAIL: _____
OTHER NOTES: _____

1) LOCATION: NOTES:

Is it easy to get to this venu? Y / N

In a centralized area?(Such as Downtown) Y / N

Is it a safe area (Shootings, etc.)? Y / N

Does it have off-duty officers? Y / N

Are the parking areas secure and safe? Y / N

Average cost of parking? $

Free valet parking? If not, cost? Y / N

Sufficient parking for your crowd?
"Extremely Important"

2) VENUE:
Hours of Operation: _____

Ages? 18+/ 21+/Teen Night: _____

Cost to use venue: _____

Venue's online Rep? (Scams, Bad Rep, etc.): _____

Cover Charge: _____

Theme Nights:	Mon:	Tue:	Wed:	Thurs:
	Fri:	Sat:	Sun:	
Busiest Night:				
Drink Specials:	Mon:	Tue:	Wed:	Thurs:
	Fri:	Sat:	Sun:	
VIP Bottle Specials:	Mon:	Tue:	Wed:	Thurs:
	Fri:	Sat:	Sun:	

Working Kitchen: Y / N

Food Available: Y / N

Presentation of Venue:

Interior design, flow, wear and tear

Exterior appeal, cleanliness, and lighting?

VIP area clean, well-maintained, furniture, etc.?

Equipment (sound, lighting, DJ plug-ins, etc.)?

Extras: Photographers, dancers, flowers, etc.?

Deposit for Venue:

Permits, licenses, fees etc:

Flexibility of Owner for negations?

Other Notes:

18 OR 21 and Over

The responsibility of checking IDs and making sure that no underage drinking occurs typically falls on the venue and the owner. Many venues don't like offering 18+ because of the potential risks involved. If you happen to have an event at an 18+ venue, you would normally charge a higher cover fee for anyone 18-20 years old. Since they can't buy alcohol, the cover charge is the main way the venue will get paid for them. Because of this, the venue may negotiate a percent fee of each cover charge for 18-20-year-olds.

Your main focus is packing the party, and having those extra bodies in the venue helps to create more energy and excitement. The longer the line outside, the more people will be interested in what's happening inside. Typically, 18 and over nights are a Ladies' Night or College Night-type crowd. Always cater your event to the women who show up. They will make or break your event.

Make sure you have a way to distinguish who is 18-20 and who is over 21 with wristbands, markers, stamps, etc. Make sure you and the owner have a clear understanding in you contract about who is responsible for checking IDs. If it's you, make sure you hire someone with experience to check IDs. Fake IDs can be purchased online or made pretty easily. Doing some basic research online about spotting fake IDs is highly recommended.

VIP AREAS & RESERVATIONS

Some promoters work out deals with the owner or manager to receive 10-15% of the total sales or bottle sales from any VIP tables that they book for the venue. Depending on the type of venue, this may or may not be a viable revenue option. There have been many nights that we've opted to buy bottles at the bar with the bartender as our server/waitress. This is a great way to make the venue look busier and create more energy at the bar where more guests can be involved. You could even offer a bottle special if someone chooses to be served at the bar instead of in the VIP area. This is also a great option when offering bachelorette parties, a "free bottle" promotion. It keeps the group around other guests who might offer to buy drinks or other bottles for the group.

Some owners might start trying to short-change you on your VIP commissions if they see you being very successful. You can always ask your VIP customers for a copy of their receipt, if they are good friends, or ask the owner/manager to see the receipts from all of your reservations. When an owner starts trying to penny-pinch, that's a big red flag for you. Keep an eye on your business, watch everything, and you might even want to start looking for a different venue for your event.

SPONSORS AND SPONSORSHIPS

Sponsors and sponsorships provide many benefits not only to your event but also to your brand. Once you have decided on the type of event you want to have and the performer(s)- DJ's, artists, bands, or shows, you need to make a list of business types that might go well with your event.

For example, if you are starting a "Salsa Saturday" party, you would want to approach some local salsa schools to see if they might be willing to do a performance, provide free lessons at an earlier time, or figure out some other mutually beneficial agreement.

If you have decided to have "Tequila Tuesday's," you could approach the venue and their liquor rep to work on deals for tequila drink specials, maybe some complimentary bottles, or a fee for advertising and promoting certain tequila brands on your promotional materials.

Sponsors play an essential role in adding credibility to your event and company. Having a brand with name recognition like Parton, Grey Goose, Johnny Walker, etc., will draw people to your party, not only because of the quality drink specials but those brands are associated with a certain perception of what the event might be like.

You could also strike a deal regarding rental sound equipment, if the need arises. Approach the vendor and offer a partnership, free use of the equipment in exchange for free advertising at the party.

The bottom line is that every sponsor or sponsorship you acquire for your event or party should either save you money and/or make you money. Remember that when a company chooses to partner on a sponsorship, they will also be promoting your party and your company.

Maintaining these relationships is key to your success. As your brand grows, those sponsors will offer more lucrative opportunities that will bring some exposure and credibility to your brand.

If you have a good relationship with liquor reps, when their companies sponsor or host much larger event and concert, they could recommend your promotions company and services to the people throwing the larger party or concert.

These opportunities come over time. Your professionalism, hospitality, and work ethic will provide you many opportunities with many different sponsors for all of your events.

TEEN NIGHT EVENTS/PARTIES

The knowledge that you will gain throughout this book is beneficial not only for you but also for your kids. A huge market in this industry is throwing teen night events/parties. This is something that you can do with your son or daughter to teach them how to handle and build a successful business.

These types of parties are usually done in the summer when school is out. Most teen are very connected and familiar with social media. This will make it easier for your teen to promote the party. To make your events or parties even bigger, you and your teen should approach other local high schools and middle schools. You want to let your teen do most of the work while you coach and guide them. Accompany your teen to meetings with school principals, venue owners, and potential sponsors. You and your teen should follow the same basic principles for promoting this event/party.

Some basic things to remember:

- Ask each school principal for permission to promote the event at that school

- Work with the school's PTA to promote the event/party and discuss any safety concerns
- Create age-appropriate flyers, posters, social media ads, and other promotional material
- Work with age-appropriate sponsors
- Offer non-alcoholic beverages and possibly food
- Set a reasonable time for the event/party (Example: 6 PM - 9PM, 7 PM - 10 PM, etc.)

The most important factor with these types of parties is safety and security. Provide a safe environment for the teens at a venue with a good reputation. You have to make sure the parents and community are on board. Promoting 90 days out from your first event/party will give you plenty of time to pack your venue. Your strategy depends on students talking about your events/parties while they are still in school. This will allow them to plan on seeing each other at these events/parties. You can also offer birthday specials, graduation specials, etc. The opportunities are endless and your creativity is your best tool in this business.

STORY: PROMOTING A "FREE NIGHT"

Let's imagine that you have no money to invest in your business but you really have the heart, drive, motivation, and determination to promote a night somewhere. The first thing we would do is our venue worksheets. We would specifically look for a venue that is slow on either Wednesdays, Thursdays, or Sundays. We would also want the venue to have a capacity of no more than 300 - 400 people. A venue of this size is easier to fill and typically won't have a cover charge on its slower nights.

While doing our venue research, we would also find out what themes are the most popular at other venues on those nights in our area. It might be Ladies' Night, Service Industry Night, or Top 40/Hip Hop Night. We would choose a theme for our night that mixes well with some of the busier venues nearby. We have decided, based on our research, that we want to start a Ladies' Night on Sundays.

Our proposal for this type of event will be a little different. Since we won't have a cover charge, we will ask the venue owner/manager to do a "bar split." Ideally, we are looking to be paid 15-20% of the bar sales after the venue's expenses. The reason we don't want a cover charge is that we are trying to draw people to a slower night at a less popular venue. Also, many people won't go out on these nights because the typically work the next day.

Once our proposal is ready, we will set up our meeting with the venue owner/manager. Be professional, respectful, and on time. We will present our proposal to the owner/manager and negotiate a fair deal that's beneficial for both parties. The owner/manager will definitely want to know about other successful events we have started or organized. Being motivated and energetic about building an awesome night at this venue will help us to close the deal and motivate the venue staff.

EVENT/PARTY PROPOSAL
Ladies' Night

We are looking to launch a new Ladies' Night at (Venue Name) on Sunday nights. Our projected opening night would be (Event Date). Our company has experience in marketing, promotions, and advertising in this area and we are interested in partnering with your venue for our new Ladies' Night.

Our goal is to attract professional women within a 20-mile radius from the venue who are ages 25-45. We will provide a safe and appealing environment where our clientele can interact with other professionals in the area. These customers will create a high-energy, profit-producing party.

We would like your venue to provide the following:

- 21 and over
- No cover charge
- Bar/security staff
- 2 drink specials that would be appealing to our clientele
- Bar split of 20%
- DJ
- In return, we will market, advertise, and promote the party over the next 60-
- 90 days in order to attract a large crowd to your venue. We will be doing the following:
- Social Media Advertising
- Purchase and distribute 10,000 flyers
- Social Media influencers with a local following
- Cross-promotions with local businesses

With our marketing plan and experience, we believe we will bring over 200 people to the grand opening of this new Ladies' Night. From our previous events and parties at other local venues, we know that our partnership for this new Ladies' Night will be mutually beneficial and exciting!

After our contract is signed with the venue, we will begin preparing our sponsorship proposal for local businesses. We want to target businesses that fit with our clientele for this party or event. Since we are doing Ladies' Night, salons, clothing stores, gyms, tanning salons, etc., would be our main focus for sponsorships. Our goal is to find at least four businesses to partner with us for some cross-promotional work. We would slightly modify our venue proposal to fit each business type.

SPONSORSHIP PROPOSAL

Ladies' Night

We are looking to launch *a* new Ladies' Night at (Venue Name) on Sunday nights. Our projected opening night would be (Event Date). Our company has experience in marketing, promotions, and advertising in this area, and we are interested in partnering with your business for this new Ladies' Night.

Our goal is to attract professional women within a 20-mile radius from the venue who are ages 25-45. We will provide a safe and appealing environment where our clientele can interact with other professionals in the area. These customers will create a high-energy, profit-producing party.

We will be doing to the following promotional work:

- Purchasing and distributing between 5,000-10,000 flyers
- Establish effective social media campaigns targeted to local professionals in our target market
- Utilize social media influencers in our area with ties to large groups of our target clientele

As party sponsor, your business would be featured on all promotional material:

- Flyers
- Posters
- Social Media campaigns

We would also like to host at least one cross-promotional event with your business at your location. Our basic sponsorship fee is $300 for this new Ladies' Night on (Event Date).

If you are interested in becoming a featured sponsor with the ability to offer featured items at our Ladies' Night, the fee is just an extra $100. The space for featured sponsors for this event is limited to just 2 businesses.

With this simple proposal, some hard work, and dedication, we were able to sign on 3 businesses at the basic level and 1 business as a featured sponsor. That's a total of $1,500 that we now have to promote our new party. This now allows us to use about $400 to buy 10,000 flyers. We are left with $1,100 to spend on social media influencers (about $300), around $500 for our street team, and the remainder for any miscellaneous expenses.

At this point, we have all of our event details figured out and our sponsors signed on. We will have all of our promotional material designed either by us, a friend, or we will use about $100-200 from our budget for a graphics designer.

Once our promotional material is ready, we would develop our distribution strategy with our street team. As we discuss in this book, we will approach local businesses within a 30-mile radius that cater to our target market, in this case women, for our Ladies' Night.

Since we are looking to pack a venue that holds about 400 people, our distribution strategy would look something like:

First 4 Weeks - 750 flyers per week to:

- Nail Salons
- Tanning Salons

- Women's Clothing Stores, or Similar Locations

Last 4 Weeks - 1,750 flyers per week to the same businesses, but:

- Include parking lots of other venues doing Ladies' Nights

- Other busy venues throughout the week

We would also use a simple tracking sheet to monitor which businesses hand out the most flyers. The feedback from these businesses will help us in the future with other events. We can figure out which events or parties are compatible with which businesses in our area.

PROMOTIONAL MATERIAL DISTRIBUTION TRACKING SHEET

EVENT: __LADIES' NIGHT (SAMPLE)__   STREET TEAM MEMBERS: Annie Jones, Billy Smith
VENUE NAME: _____   ADDRESS: _____
NIGHT OF WEEK Sun   _____
MUSIC TYPE: Top 40   _____
NOTES _____   _____

BUSINESS INFO	DATE(S)	# OF FLYERS
NAME: Alexis' Nails	3/25/21	100
ADDRESS:	4/02/21	80
Manager:	Notes:	
NAME: Giana's Tans	3/25/21	100
ADDRESS:	4/02/21	125
Manager:	Notes: Asked for more flyers, and getting positive feedback!	
NAME: Miranda's Hair Salon	3/25/21	100
ADDRESS:	4/02/21	100
Manager:	Notes:	

* This form can be customized depending on how many weeks you want to represent on each page. You can also fill in all the business names and addresses ahead of time so your street team knows exactly where you want them to go.

PROMOTIONAL MATERIAL DISTRIBUTION TRACKING SHEET

EVENT: _____   STREET TEAM MEMBERS: _____

VENUE NAME: _____   ADDRESS: _____

NIGHT OF WEEK: _____   _____

MUSIC TYPE: _____   _____

NOTES: _____

BUSINESS INFO   DATE(S)   # OF FLYERS

NAME: _____   _____   _____

ADDRESS: _____   _____   _____

_____   _____   _____

Manager: _____   Notes: _____

_____

NAME: _____   _____   _____

ADDRESS: _____   _____   _____

_____   _____   _____

Manager: _____   Notes: _____

_____

NAME: _____   _____   _____

ADDRESS: _____   _____   _____

_____   _____   _____

Manager: _____   Notes: _____

_____

* This form can be customized depending on how many weeks you want to represent on each page. You can also fill in all the business names and addresses ahead of time so your street team knows exactly where you want them to go.

〈 〉

SINCE THIS EVENT WOULDN'T have a cover charge, we wouldn't need to worry about a cashier or any door staff to help out. The night of our grand opening, we would do a walk-through of the venue, check in with the manager, and begin reaching out to our social media influencers. We would be working the street in front of the venue and even have one or two people from our street team helping to guide people to our party. This is our opportunity to shine and show the manager/owner that we are serious about having a party.

At the end of the night, we would check with the venue's door staff to see how many people showed up. For this example, let's say that we got 250 people to show up at the venue for our grand opening. On average, people spend at least $25 per person at a bar or nightclub when they go out. Based on this average, the venue made about $6,250 at the bar. The DJ may have cost the venue $500, and they probably spent about the same amount for staffing. That would leave $5,250, and since we negotiated a 20% split, we would be paid $1,050 for the night, plus $200 left over from the sponsorship money. That's a total of $1,250! Not too bad considering that you started with $0 for your business budget!

Now, we would keep pushing and promoting for the next Sunday and drive up those bar sales even more to make more money.

《 》

EVENT: LADIES NIGHT (SAMPLE)

OPENING DATE: / /

VENUE: _____

ADDRESS _____

_____

_____

EXPENSES

BUDGET AVAILABLE: $ 0 . . . .

NOTES: _____

_____

_____

_____

EXPENDITURES

1) VENUE: _____

_____

2) FLYERS/POSTERS: $ 4 0 0 _ _ _ _ _ _ _

3) STREET TEAM $500- - - - - - - - - -

4) RADIO: . . . .

5) TV . . . .

11) WRISTBANDS: _____

12) DECORATIONS: _____

13) GIVEAWAYS: _____

14) EQUIPMENT RENTALS: _____

15) PERMITS & LICENSES: _____

6) DJ/TALENT/RIDER: _____

7) CASHIER/VIP CASHIER: _____

8) GRAPHICS DESIGN: $100

9) SOCIAL MEDIA: Influencers: $300

16) MERCHANDISE: _____

17) MISCELANEOUS _____

BUD

BUDGET: $ 0

TOTAL EXPENSES: $ 1,300

OVER/UNDER BUDGET: $ - 1,300

. . .

10) SECURITY: ....

INCOMES

1) COVER CHARGE: _____

2) BAR SPLIT 1,050

3) SPONSORSHIPS: 1,500

4) MERCHANDISE: _____

5) TICKET SALES: _____

6) MISCELANEOUS: _____

TOTAL INCOME: $2550

TOTAL INCOME: $ 2500

TOTAL EXPENSES: $ 1300

TOTAL PROFIT: $ 1250

PART III

DESIGNING FLYERS, POSTERS, AND MARKETING MATERIALS

You could plan the best event in the world, but if you can't get people to show up, none of your hard work will matter. One very important aspect of having a successful event or party is great promotional materials and designs. This material is your event's "image" to your clientele and potential customer base. The colors you choose, design features, catch-phrases, drink specials, talent, and the event's atmosphere all need to flow together on your flyers, posters, and banners. Your promotional tools are what will draw people to your event or party and get them to pay your cover charge. We are going to review some key points in preparing your promotional material before we discuss the best ways to get this material out to the public.

The main focus of your promotional material is to entice people to come out for your event. Your promo material should be reflective of the type of event you are having. If you are doing a Valentine's Day Party, your promo material should have hearts, roses, chocolates, or other relevant imagery. If you are doing a "Free" roses giveaway to the ladies, having a bunch of roses on your material is obviously a good idea. Using reds, pinks, and white as your promo material colors works well with a Valentine's Day theme. Your event specials or featured guests' names should be the most prominent components of the material.

If you are doing a concert or having a celebrity guest appearance at your event, you should list all of the performances and maybe some of their most popular songs. Have pictures of the performers, maybe some of their famous tweets or sayings on the material. You can also ask the celebrity or performers for images or promo material that you can add to your campaign.

When designing promo material for a regular weekly event, you have to be a little more creative. Your promo material can change slightly from month to month or when you are doing special giveaways or other promos on that night. If you are starting a Salsa Saturday, you would obviously have images of people dancing salsa on the flyer. You could use reds, yellows, orange, and white for your color combos. Highlight your drink specials, if any, or if there is a "Latin inspired" martini or shot that is available. You might have a salsa dance school featured for the first month and run a different salsa feature for the following month. Let your creativity run wild! You will learn over time what promo material works best for you and your clientele.

Creativity is key. Your clientele has seen hundreds of flyers and posters. The same basic designs are all reused by different venues and promoters in every city. Make yours stand out. Your budget will also affect what your options are regarding flyer size, finish, quantity, and style. If you are tight on cash, you could probably design something yourself with a little time, research and experience. If you can afford it, you could hire a graphic designer to help you out. Sometimes you can work out a deal with the designer to get the artwork for free. You could put the designer's logo

and contact information in your promo material or offer them free cover at the party. For examples of flyers and promo materials, research the other events and parties in your area.

CATCH-PHRASES AND EVENT NAMES

Naming your event or party and using catch-phrases that will draw people to your event are two important factors for your promo campaign. Something that is easy and fun to remember will make your promotional strategy even more powerful.

Here are a few "catchy" event or party names that we have used:

- Fresh Fridays - Hip-Hop Night
- Salsa Saturdays - Latin Night
- Wine Down Wednesdays - Mid-week Wine Happy Hour
- Freaky Fridays - Top 40/Hip Hop Night
- Free Fridays - if you have no cover until 10:30PM
- Ladies' Night - any night with a focus on specials for ladies like free cover, drink specials, etc.
- College Night - might be 18+ for that night

- Service Industry – Specials for bar/nightclub workers - - Usually on Sundays or Mondays

- Tequila Tuesdays/Thursdays - tequila specials
- Pride Party - LGBTQ events
- Sultry Saturdays - Lingerie inspired Saturday party

The possibilities are endless and your creativity is what will draw people to your event.

FLYER SIZES

The most common flyer sizes are the quarter page and the business card. The quarter page sized flyer is usually the one distributed at local businesses or after an event ends and placed on cars in parking lots. The business card sized flyer is better for when you are doing hand-to-hand promotions at business mixers, happy hours, or other local events. A business card sized flyer is easier for someone to put in their pocket. They are less likely to throw it away.

PICKING YOUR STREET TEAM

Now that you have flyers and promo material designed, you need your street team to begin promoting your event. There are a few different ways you can find good people for a promotional street team.

College students are a good option because they usually like to party and always need extra cash. College students usually have a large network of friends to promote to, as well. The downside to college students is that they can be lazy or may not show up.

Students or interns at broadcasting schools or who are in marketing majors or programs. Many of them need intern hours, extra intern hours, or volunteer hours. Most will work for free as long as you pay for their gas and food. It's also wise to invite these students to your party and let them and a small group in for free, like 2-3 people each.

Radio stations typically use street teams and once you build a relationship with a radio station, some of their street team members might be willing to work for you also. It's an easy way to earn extra cash and perks.

Ultimately, your goal in hiring people for your street team is to find motivated, energetic, outgoing, and independent individuals who get excited about your parties and events.

WORKING WITH YOUR STREET TEAM

Once you have hired your street team, you will arrange a meeting with all of them. Always introduce yourself first and let them know what event they will be promoting. You want to discuss their pay, perks, hours, and job responsibilities.

It is important to get feedback from your street team so that they can feel involved in the promotional process. The more vested they are in your event, the harder they will work to make it a success. Explain who your target market is, what date the event is planned for, and which venue the event or party is being held at.

Ask your street team for their feedback on the venue. Write down their responses. If it's negative feedback, make sure they tell you the whole story. These things might be obstacles for your event that you have to overcome.

As an example, if we were to do a hip-hop party at a nightclub downtown, our goal would be to target a 30-mile radius from the venue. At the street team meeting, we would research and list every barbershop, hair salon, nail salon, clothing store, restaurant, car wash, tanning salon, nutrition store, cell phone shop, jewelry store, and any other business where our targeted clients might frequent. Some of the people on your street team might have connections at some of these types of businesses. These connections are great opportunities for potential sponsorships or small promotional events to boost exposure for the business and your event or party.

Once you have all of the businesses listed, work with your street team to break the locations up into groups of 10-20 businesses. Assign the groups to your street team along with a schedule to pass out flyers and posters. You should be sending your street team to these locations at least twice prior to your event's launch.

Explain to your street team that as they visit each of these businesses, they should introduce themselves, be polite, and ask for permission to leave a stack of flyers and business cards. Depending on the type of event, you could also have your street team hand out VIP tickets or admission to the business owner or manager. This can encourage the owner/manager to show up with some of the employees and to also hype the event for you. Networking is a huge asset to your success. Every business that supports you is a powerful tool for future events and parties.

The next step is to discuss with your street team any clubs, bars, or other venues that have good crowds with the same type of clientele you are looking to attract. You can also write down the venue's cover charge, drink specials, or other promotions. Here is an example:

- Mondays: The Blue Whale

2-for-1 drinks 8-1O PM with no cover until 11 PM

- Tuesdays: Mike's Lounge

$4 Corona, ½ price VIP bottles with no cover all night

- Wednesdays: Chillers

$2 shots until 11 PM and $2 Bud Light all night

- Thursdays: Excite Dance Club

College Night, 18 and over, no cover for ladies until 11 PM
3-for-1 until midnight

- Fridays: Loud House

$100 Hennessy bottles, $5 cover until 11PM
2-for-1 "Incredible Hulk" drinks

- Saturdays: Baila (Dance)

Latin night with salsa music, 2-for-1 tequila shots

DISTRIBUTION STRATEGIES

Once you have compiled this list, create another schedule for your street team based on the most popular nights at these venues. Use your resources wisely. On the busiest nights at each of these venues, you will have your team distributing your flyers onto all of the cars in the parking lots and/or garages nearby. You will start your flyer distribution schedule about 60 days prior to your event's grand opening. You can also have your street team walking up and down the sidewalks near those busy venues, handing out business card sized flyers. Large entertainment districts are great places for hand to hand distribution. It also provides an opportunity for your street team to connect with some potential clients.

VERY IMPORTANT

NEVER SEND YOUR STREET TEAM INSIDE ANY VENUE TO HAND OUT ANY PROMOTIONAL MATERIAL. This is a huge industry NO-NO. This can cause you problems with other promoters and venue owners/managers. Usually, parking lots and garages, streets, and public areas are fair game for handing out promo material. Some smaller venues may have an issue with you passing out flyers in their own parking lots.

The best times to distribute flyers to local businesses are usually around lunch time, in the afternoon, or maybe a slower part of the day. You want some time to speak to the business owners/managers for 5-10 minutes. This will help build some rapport and set a good tone for your party or event. When handing out flyers at night near the busiest venues, you should target a time about an hour or two before the venue closes. This is an ideal time to put flyers on the vehicles so that they won't be removed. For hand-to-hand distribution, you can have your team walk around for about an hour prior to hitting the parking lots and garages.

When your street team goes out to canvas an area, it is best to go with them. You need to be distributing flyers, business cards, and other promo material as well. You will set the example for your street team. Once they see how hard you work, they will recognize that you are serious. This is also a great way to keep your team accountable for their distribution area. If your teams break into small groups to hit larger areas, you need to have them write down where they went, who they spoke to, and if they got any feedback about your flyers or the event. These notes are good so you can visit those locations later to verify that your team actually did their job. If you send your team to flyer a parking lot, do a drive-by later on to verify that they handed out all the material.

It is unfortunate that you have to verify your team's work, but it is necessary until you build a team that you can trust. Many times, we have witnessed people claiming that they canvassed an area, but they instead put your flyers in the trash somewhere. Every flyer wasted is a dollar lost from your pocket.

Keep in mind that if you are doing a smaller event, you should be able to handle flyer distribution on your own. This saves you money and you make sure the job is done right. This also allows you to get a feel for what your potential clientele are looking for in an event.

EXAMPLE EVENT/PARTY: COLLEGE NIGHT PARTY

As a promoter, your first job is to promote and organize a successful event. Of course, you will hire people to help you promote, but a real promoter has a lot of work to do. This is where you have to be serious about building your business. As an example, we are going to describe how we would organize and promote an event. First, you must decide on what type of event you want to have, as we have previously discussed. Let's imagine that you are going to start a Top 40 College Night that is 18 and over.

You should do your research to find out which clubs will host 18 and over nights in an area with at least one big university nearby. If there are multiple community colleges and universities in a concentrated area, that's even better. We would look for a venue that isn't very busy on Friday or Saturday nights. This type of venue would be in desperate need of a promoter or a fresh spin on their current promotions. Let's start with a $2,500 budget for your event, and the venue holds about 1,000 people. Arrange a meeting with the owner/manager and follow the steps from earlier in this book. We would attempt to negotiate a $500 rental fee for the venue that will include all security, bartenders, and waitresses. Some venues might be more expensive to rent, but since this venue isn't busy and needs help, they should be willing to negotiate a fair price. Make sure the venue owner/manager understands that you are spending your personal money on advertising, promotional material, and the DJ or entertainment. What you want from the deal is full control of the door revenue. Since you know that the venue owner/manager won't make any money from guests under 21, offer 25% of the "under 21" cover charges to the owner. This is a sign of good business practices on your part. The owner/manager might negotiate this point, but be mindful that you are helping them.

Once you have your agreement in place with the venue, set your event/party grand opening date. This date should be at least 60 days, but preferably 80-90 days, from the day of your signed agreement with the venue. You should also pay your $500 rental fee in advance to show that you mean business. This also locks in your opening date and binds the venue to your agreement.

Your next step would be to hire a well-known local DJ that has a pretty good following in the area. Contact several DJs and get their rates for doing either a few hours at your event, or the whole night. Make your best choice based on the DJ's credentials, following, social media presence, and your budget. You can also hire a lesser-known DJ from one of the surrounding colleges or universities to fill in for the times that your main DJ may not be performing.

Your target should be to spend between $500-$800 on DJs and entertainment. If you lock the main DJ in as your resident DJ for the event, they might be willing to give you a discounted rate, but as long as your DJ has a good following that will show up, the money spent will be make up for on the cover charge. Once your venue, opening date, and DJ are locked in, it's time to work on your promotional material and marketing strategy.

Since your budget was only $2,500 to start with, and you have already set aside $500 for your DJ and spent another $500 on the venue rental, you have $1,500 left to pack your event!

We want to hire a street team to distribute our promotional material as the basis of our strategy, but we will discuss street teams in greater detail later on in this book. As part of the interview process with your potential street team members, and before the first street team meeting ever takes place, you should find out if any of them have connections with local businesses. If they do, that's great news, but the team members should NEVER do any business for the promoter or on your behalf. YOU (the promoter) should go to each of these businesses yourself and work out deals for sponsorships. The street team's only job is to distribute flyers, posters and help with social media, but if a member of your team does have these connections, invite them along when you visit the business. This may help win the opportunity to explain your event to the owner or manager and explore the possibility of partnerships for promotional material.

After hiring your street team, you want to approach local businesses for potential event/party sponsorships. When speaking with each business owner/manager, explain that you and your street team will be distributing about 10,000 flyers over the next 60-90 days. Review your sponsorship proposal with the owner/manager to highlight the benefits of a partnership. Ask the business for $300 to help pay for the materials, flyer distribution, and to add their info to the flyer. If you can get four businesses to partner up at $300 each, that's an extra $1,200 for your marketing budget. If you can acquire 10,000 flyers for about $400, you would have the reminder to pay your street team for distribution. If you were able to hire all interns for your street team, you could save most of that $800 since those interns are getting hours towards their school programs.

Keep in mind that to legally be able to assign credit hours to interns and students, you will have to have your promotional company established as either an LLC, S-Corp, C-Corp, or any other legal entity. Check the laws and regulations in your state. It is crucial that those interns get the proper credit thy earn. If something goes wrong, they could bad-mouth your event and company.

When your promo material is completed, organize your street team and assign groups of local businesses and venues with a schedule for each street member. Since we are building a college night, make sure you target all of the local colleges and universities. Establish your social media presence using Facebook, Instagram, and Twitter, or any other high-traffic sites. You can also approach some of the more popular students at the colleges and universities, offering to pay them $50-$100 for promoting your event on campus. If you hire 2-4 students, that's $100-$400. Use your best judgment to work out a fair deal. This leaves you with between $400-$700 for your street team, plus the $1,500 from your original budget.

On the day of the event, we would usually go and do a soundcheck to make sure all the equipment is working. We would also bring a cashier and a door person if needed. Always bring your own cashier. DO NOT TRUST ANYONE from the venue with YOUR money. Do a walk-through of the venue to see if there are any side doors where people can sneak in and out of. There shouldn't be any issues, but if people sneak in, that's money out of your pocket.

During the walk-through, it is also important to have the venue owner/ manager make clear to their staff that they cannot get anyone in for free. This is your night and the door is for you. You will still have venue staff trying to bully your cashier or door person, but by addressing this issue early on, it should minimize the problem. Once your staff is in place, the venue prepped, and your DJ/entertainment set up, you are ready to go! Depending on how much of your budget you spent, you should be in pretty good shape. Based on this example, you would still have about $1,500 in your budget plus $400 - $700 from your business partnerships. That's a total of $1,900 - $2,200 left over. If about 500 people show up for your party, at an average cover charge of $10, your gross will be $5,000! Of course, you now have to subtract your expenses.

EXPENSE/ INCOME SHEET

College Night

Event/Party Name   College Night   Budget Available: $2,500

Opening Date   Notes:

Venue Name

Address:

Expenses: **Income:**

    Venue $500   Sponsorships: $1,200

    Flyers/Posters   400   Cover Charge: 5,000

    Street Team   400   **TOTAL: $6,200**

    DJ   500

    Cashier   125

    Social Media

Influencer: 200

    Social Media

       Advertisers: 300

Security Staff: 100

TOTAL: **$2525**

Total Income: **$6,200**

Total Expenses: *2,525*

Total Profits: **$3,675**

    This is just an example to get you familiar with some of the process. Throughout this book, we will cover all of the topics mentioned in this story. Think about how you would promote this College Night somewhere near you.

EVENT/PARTY PROPOSAL

College Night

We are looking to launch a new College Night at (Venue Name) on Saturday night's. Our projected opening night would be (Event Date). Our company has experience in marketing, promotions, and advertising in this area, and we are interested in working with your venue for our new College Night.

Our goal is to attract local students from the nearby colleges and universities. Our customers will be 18 and over and looking for a new party to build as their own. Most of these local students will be members of fraternities and sororities or heavily involved in campus activities. We will bring these customers to your venue for a high energy, profit-producing party.

We would like your venue to provide the following:

- 18 and over
- DJ
- Bar/security staff
- 2-for-1 drink special on vodka and tequila
- Venue rental fee of $500
- We will have full control of door revenue with a 25% fee to the venue for each 18-20 admission

In return, we will market, advertise, and promote the event over the next 60-90 days in order to attract a large crowd to your venue. We will be doing the following:

- Pay a $500 rental fee upon signing the business agreement
- Supply a featured DJ
- Purchase and distribute 10,000 flyers
- Social Media marketing campaigns
- Social Media/Campus Influencers

- Strategic business partnerships to boost credibility for the event
- Provide cashier

With our marketing plan and experience, we believe that we will bring over 500 people to the grand opening of this new College Night. From our previous events and parties at other local venues, we know that our partnership for this new College Night will be mutually beneficial and exciting!

SPONSORSHIP PROPOSAL

College Night

We are launching a new College Night at (Venue Name) on Saturday nights. Our projected opening night is (Event Date). Our company has extensive experience in marketing, advertising, and promotions in this area and we are interested in partnering with you for this new College Night.

Our target market is local college and university students between the ages of 18-24 who want a hip, new venue to party at. These local students will be members of fraternities and sororities and heavily involved in campus activities. We believe that a partnership with your company would be mutually beneficial and profitable for everyone involved. We will be doing the following promotional work:

- Purchasing and distributing over 10,000 flyers
- Establish effective social media campaigns targeted to local colleges and universities
- Utilize local social media influencers in our target market with ties to local colleges and universities
- Cross-promotional work with our featured DJ

As an event sponsor, your business would be featured on all promotional material:

- Flyers
- Posters
- Social Media campaigns

We would also like to host at least one cross-promotional event with your business at your location. Our basic sponsorship fee is $300 for this new College Night on (Event Date). If you are interested in becoming a featured sponsor with the ability to offer featured items at our College Night, the fee is just an extra $200. The space for featured sponsors for this event is limited to just 2 businesses.

PART IV

VENUE MEETING BEFORE OPENING

Typically, about an hour or two before the opening of your event, you should arrive at the venue with your cashier, equipment, and any door staff you need. Your equipment might include your own cash register, cash box, electronic payment system, door clicker, wristbands, and any promotional material for your next event. This is a meeting that you would have with the owner or manager in order to introduce your staff to the venue staff. If there's an agreed-upon "Free Admission" list for the venue, they would give it to you at this time or prior to the meeting. At this point, the owner/manager should have made clear to their staff that unless a guest is on that list, they MUST pay the cover charge, if there is one. Also, take this time to do a walk-through of the venue, get your staff in place, and setup your equipment. Confirm your schedule with the DJ and prep anything that they might need.

If you are going to be utilizing a street team during the event to pull people from the streets to your party or to distribute flyers, you would normally have them arrive at the venue right around opening time. You would then give them instructions based on what your event needs are.

Keep in mind that if your event is at a stand-alone venue with no other "nightlife" businesses around, you won't be able to use your street team to pull people to your opening night. They are still able to distribute flyers later on in the evening on vehicles near the busiest venues. Have your plan in place BEFORE the venue opens.

DURING THE EVENT

Prior to opening the venue, you should have a rough idea as to how many people to expect based on your marketing and promotional work. If you properly distributed 5,000 flyers, you could expect about 250 people based on the industry standard return of 5%. If you are using social media influencers, you should have an estimate from them as to how many people will be coming with them. Your DJ might have a group of loyal followers that show up. There are many techniques and strategies that we have covered in this book that will help bring people to your event if followed correctly.

While your event is open, you want to be accessible to your cashier and door staff, but you don't want to hang out at the door all night. If your friends see you at the door, they are going to ask for free cover, or they might make a scene if they don't get in for free. Do your best to STAY AWAY FROM THE CASHIER and just let your staff do the job they are being paid to do.

If you are using a street team to pull people from sidewalks or near other venues, go out there with them. You can offer a bonus to your street team if they bring a certain number of people to the venue. As an example, tell them that each person who brings 25 people to the party gets a $50 or $100 bonus. They might invite more friends or people that they know, but that's fine since those people are paying your cover charge, too.

If there are any issues at the door, your cashier and door staff should have the backing of the manager on duty. If it's a serious issue or discrepancy, always be available via your phone or show up at the venue door to handle the problem.

THE MOST IMPORTANT THING: DO NOT GET DRUNK!!!

This will cost you money, affect your reputation with the venue owner/manager, and very likely will cause problems. We have both lost money doing events and parties. Almost every time, it was because we got drunk and didn't manage our staff and the event properly. If you remember only one thing from this book, make sure it's this.

Throughout the night, about every hour, you should go by the front door and collect your cash. Verify the number of people who have entered against how much money you collect every hour. We have provided these sample worksheets for this purpose.

CASH PICKUP/TRACKING SHEET

Venue: Cover Charge:
Date: Cashier Name:
Door Staff:

TIME:	11PM	12AM	12:30AM	1AM	1:30AM	2AM
$/Amt:						
II/Guests:						

EXAMPLE: $10 cover

TIME:	11PM	12AM	12:30AM
$/Amt:	$800	$1,560	$2,380
#/Guests:	80	234	478

To verify that your cashier isn't stealing, verify the number of guests and the amount of money collected. 80 guests x $10 cover= $800, so everything is good. You collected $800 from the cashier at 11 PM and $1,560 at 12 AM; your total is $2,360. If there are 234 people in the venue at 12 AM, then do your calculation. 234 x $10 = $2,340, since you collected $2,360, no one has stolen from you, but the door count isn't correct. At 12:30 AM, you collect $2,380 and add that to the $2,360 that was collected earlier, for a total now of $4,740. The count now is 478, so our math is 478 x $10 = $4780, which is $40 short. This could mean that the cashier is stealing or the door staff counted too many people. In either case, you must decide how to handle the situation. People do make mistakes, but they must also be held accountable for their actions. Trust your gut.

《 》

CASH PICKUP/TRACKING SHEET

DATE:VENUE:

COVER: $_____   CASHIER NAME:

                        DOOR STAFF

TIME:	11PM	11:30	12AM	12:30	1AM	1:30	2AM	CLOSE
$/AMT:								
#/GUESTS:								

TOTAL COLLECTED: $ _____   TOTAL GUESTS

GUESTS x COVER CHARGE= $_____

CASH PICKUP/TRACKING SHEET

DATE:

VENUE: CASHIER NAME:

COVER: $ _____   DOOR STAFF:

TIME:	11PM	11:30	12AM	12:30	1AM	1:30	2AM	CLOSE
$/AMT:								
#/GUESTS:								

TOTAL COLLECTED: $_____   TOTAL GUESTS:

GUESTS x COVER CHARGE= $_____

CASH PICKUP/TRACKING SHEET

DATE:

VENUE: CASHIER NAME:

COVER: $_____   DOOR STAFF:

TIME:	11PM	11:30	12AM	12:30	1AM	1:30	2AM	CLOSE
$/AMT:								
#/GUESTS:								

TOTAL COLLECTED: $ _____   TOTAL GUESTS:

// GUESTS x COVER CHARGE = $_____

CLOSING OUT THE NIGHT

About 30 minutes before your event or party ends, you should be preparing your payouts for your DJ, cashier, door staff, street team, and anyone else that worked for you that night. Paying your people the night of says a lot about your professionalism, integrity, and business. Keeping your employees happy will build your business just as much as most of the other techniques mentioned in this book.

PROMOTING YOUR NEXT EVENT

The last necessary piece of this event or party is to make sure to promote your next one. About an hour before closing, the cashier and door staff should be handing out flyers for the next event. The DJ should also be doing shout-outs advertising your next event. If you can collect emails or business cards to build your clientele database, even better. Every little thing you do adds up!

Our last story for you is an example of a large concert. We have thrown concerts like this and have made six figures almost every time. It takes a lot of hard work, but by using all of the tools in this book, you can achieve this level of success as well.

EXAMPLE EVENT PARTY: PROMOTING A HIP-HOP CONCERT

Let's imagine that we are going to organize and promote a Hip-Hop concert. Our budget for this event is $50,000. We are planning to sell our concert tickets for $40 each. One of the first things we must do is find a suitable venue for the concert. In this instance, we are looking for a venue that holds between 3,000 to 4,000 people. Using the venue worksheet from this book, we would create a list of all our potential venues for this concert. We would then contact each venue to see what event dates are available approximately 4-6 months from today. While speaking with each venue, we would be asking how much they charge for having a concert at their venue and what is included in that price. Based on this information, we would create a new list in order to compare the venues with each other.

List of possible venues:

House of Jazz:
Capacity - 3,500
Rental fee - $10,000
Available Dates - May 4-5, 26-28
Rental fee includes: all staff, off-duty officers, ticket collectors, VIP area

Elixir:
Capacity - 4,000
Rental fee - $7,500
Available Dates - May 5, 26-28
Rental fee includes: staff, free parking, off-duty officers, assistance for ticket sales, VIP

Bricks:
Capacity - 3,250
Rental fee - $8,000
Available Dates - May 4, 11-12, 26
Rental fee includes: all staff, VIP area

After reviewing our list and using the venue worksheets, we have decided to use Elixir as our concert venue. We would then contact Elixir again to finalize the contract details and add some stipulations that the concert be 18 and over and anyone 13 and up could attend with an adult. Obviously, we negotiate that we receive 100% of all ticket sales and door revenue. Typically, upon signing our contract with the venue, we would have to pay either the whole rental fee or a non-refundable deposit.

EVENT/PARTY PROPOSAL

Hip-Hop Concert

We are looking to promote a large Hip-Hop Concert at Elixir on May 27th. Our company has extensive experience in marketing, promotions, and advertising in this area and we are interested in renting your venue for this concert.

What we are looking for from your venue:

- 18 and over admission
- 13 and over with an adult
- We keep 100% of all ticket sales
- Full door staff, security, bar staff, waitresses, etc.
- Lighting and sound technician
- All lighting and sound equipment provided
- At least 2 off-duty officers
- Hours of Operation: 7 PM - 10 PM

We will pay a non-refundable deposit upon signing an agreement with your venue.

Note that this event/party proposal is a little different and much more direct. We are paying to rent the venue with all staff for a one-night concert. We will negotiate the cost, however, what we do for marketing and advertising doesn't really matter to the venue owner/manager. We have to pay our fees regardless of whether the venue is packed or not.

Once we have locked in our venue and concert date, we will begin researching potential artists. We want artists with good social media followings and who might be up and coming with a new hit track. Our goal is to find 3- 4 artists that fit our budget for entertainment, which is $15,000 - 20,000. Finding out the artists' average working fee without contacting a booking agent is ideal. If you just give your budget numbers to a booking agent, they will usually add a few thousand dollars to the artist's actual fee and keep the extra cash. Once we have all our artists' information, we will begin contacting booking agents to see who can get us the best deals.

In this example, the booking agent got us a well-known artist for $17,500 and an up-and-coming artist for $7,500. The booking agent would then send over the contracts to finalize the deal. A few stipulations that we want to include in the contract are the following:

- the artists make a two hour after-party appearance at a venue of our choice

- live radio interview on the day of the event

- two voice recordings saying that he/she will be performing at whatever venue, and also appearing wherever for the after-party for use in the radio spots

Many artists and celebrities have what's called a Rider included with their contracts. A Rider is a special request list for the artists or celebrities. It could include things like:

- certain types of candy (only RED Mike & Ike's or BLUE M&Ms)
- special cookies or desserts (macaroons or double fudge brownies)
- certain sodas or beverages (Red Bull or Fanta, etc.)

We would typically set aside about $300 - $500 for the Rider in our budget. Most artist or celebrity contracts. Also include that we pay for airfare, hotel rooms, and transportation for them and their small entourage. Reserving the airfare, rooms, and transportation ahead of time will save us money. Usually, we have to pay the artist or celebrity 50% of their fee upon signing the contract. The other half is paid the day of the event. Many artists or celebrities won't leave their rooms until they are paid the second half of their fee.

Currently, we have our venue booked, event date set, and our artists locked in. Next, we would be booking a nightclub for the after-party. Many nightclubs will jump at the opportunity to host an after-party with well-known celebrities and artists. This gives us leverage when we negotiate our deal to rent the nightclub. The venue knows we are spending a lot of money so the event will be very well promoted. This means extra advertising for the nightclub, plus they know they will make tons of money on drinks and bottles. We would use our venue worksheets again to do our research and find the best venue for our after-party.

Let's say that we were able to rent a nightclub that holds 2,000 people for a fee of $4,000. This rental fee includes all staff, security, off-duty officers, etc. As always, we keep 100% of the door revenue and use our own cashiers and door security, if needed. We would offer the owner/manager a free admission list of 40 people total for the after-party. We would sign our contract and pay any necessary deposits.

Our next step would be to start contacting big companies, small businesses, and local shops for sponsorship opportunities. Having a large event with artists and celebrities will make it easier to attract sponsorship partners. Most business owners know that events and concerts, like in this example, would have a large portion of their budget spent on advertising and promotions. Ideally, we are targeting businesses like liquor brands, energy drink companies, and other businesses that would mix well with our target market.

When contacting these companies for potential sponsorship deals, we would set up meetings with their brand managers or reps. We would create a sponsorship proposal that would outline the benefits of the partnership.

At these meetings, present yourself in a professional manner. Always be timely, respectful, enthusiastic, and motivated. Our energy and excitement will help us close these deals. Once we have established good business relationships, more opportunities will be available for us with future events

SPONSORSHIP PROPOSAL

Substitute parenthesis in our example with your own event's information.

We are organizing, promoting, and advertising a concert with (artists/celebrities). Our event will be on (May 27th, 2022) at (Elixir) from (7 PM - 10 PM). We are also hosting an after-party at (venue name) from (11 PM -2 AM). There are (4,000) tickets available for the concert and (2,000) for the after-party.

We are looking to build a mutually beneficial business partnership with (company name). As part of a sponsorship deal with us, we will provide the following marketing and promotional opportunities:

(Company Name and/or Logo) will be featured on all of our flyers, posters, and other promotional materials distributed within a 30-mile radius. This includes:

- 35,000 flyers
- 500 posters
- Radio advertising
- TV commercials
- T-shirts
- Ticket stubs

It will also include social media marketing via Facebook, Instagram, Twitter, and more.

- You will be provided 5 free admission tickets to the concert and after-party.
- The ability to have your product featured at the concert and after-party. This is an extra fee and limited to 3 partners.

- (Any other special incentives you might want to offer.)

The basic sponsorship fee is $2,000 to be featured on all of our promotional materials, and this is limited to 5 partners.

If your company wants a feature product at the concert and the after-party, then the fee is $3,500 and limited to 3 partners.

Since we did a great job with our sponsorship proposal and sales pitch, we were able to sign-up 4 businesses at $2,000 and one at $3,500 with a featured tequila brand. Our total budget for our concert is now $61,500, since we just added $11,500 in sponsorship funding:

4 x $2,000 = $8,000

+1 x $3,500 =$3,500

$11,500

The next phase of our strategy would be to contact the local Hip Hop radio stations and set up meetings with their sales managers. We would modify our sponsorship proposal slightly so that we can outline exactly the type of partnership we want with the radio station. Here is an example of the modified proposal:

RADIO STATION PROPOSAL

A gain, substitute your own event's information for the examples we provide. We are organizing, promoting, and advertising a concert with (artists/celebrities). Our concert will be on (May 27th, 2022) at (Elixir) from (7 PM - 10 PM). We are also hosting an after-party at (venue name) from (11 PM - 2 AM). There are (4,000) tickets· available for the concert and (2,000) tickets for the after-party. We are looking to build a mutually beneficial business partnership with (Radio Station name). This is going to be a high-energy event with fantastic opportunities for our strategic partners to maximize the impact of this concert on our target markets.

Our promotional strategy includes featuring (radio station name) as the prominent name on all of our promotional material. Our strategy includes:

- Distribution of 35,000 flyers and 500 posters for 12 weeks prior to the concert to businesses within a 30-mile radius from (Elixir).
- Social Media campaigns
- Radio and TV commercials
- Strategic sponsorship deals and cross-promotional opportunities
- (Any other special incentives you want to offer)

Throughout our partnership with (radio station name), we are looking for the following:

- $10,000 worth of radio commercials for the concert and after-party
  $5,000 worth of social media cross-promotions for the concert and after-party
- A radio personality and DJ for the concert and after-party

- Live interview with the artists on the day of the event/concert to be aired throughout the date of the event
- Radio commercial production 84 free concert and after-party tickets to be given away, 2 weeks prior to the event
- Live call-ins

As a result of our cross-promotional efforts, we believe we will sell all of the available tickets for both the concert and after-party. We are looking to negotiate a fair price for these cross-promotional activities

As you can see, we get a little creative and aggressive with what we want from our deal. Our radio budget is about $10,000, but obviously we would still negotiate with the radio station to get the best possible deal.

Next, we would be setting up our event's Facebook page, Twitter, Instagram, and other social media accounts so that we have all of our platforms ready to promote with all of our business partnerships established. Then, we will establish our account with a ticket vendor to sell our concert and after-party tickets. We want to make sure that our link for ticket sales is on all of our social media pages and promotional materials.

Now that we have our sponsorship partners, venues, artists, radio partner, and event date established, we would contact a graphic designer. We would provide them with all of our event details, sponsors, partners, and featured products. This includes photos from the artists, sponsor logos, ticket prices, concert times, locations, etc. Once the artwork for our flyers, posters, and social media campaign is completed and signed off on, we would order five boxes of 5,000 flyers for the concert and two boxes of 5,000 flyers for the concert and after-party. These 10,000 flyers would be double-sided, mentioning the concert on one side and the after-party on the other. We would order about 500 posters or about $200 - $1000 worth of posters. Our total cost for the flyers should be around $200 per box, so $200 x 7 = $1,400. Plus, $200-$1000 for the posters. The total cost would be between $1,600 and $2,400.

Using TV commercials might seem outdated but it still plays a role in exposing our target market to the concert and after-party information. We would set up a meeting with local stations and speak with their sales managers. This process is much easier than with the radio stations, believe it or not. We are just trying to purchase about $2,500 worth of TV commercials. Typically, the sales manager will know the market demographics and the best strategy for how to use our budget. Most TV stations will produce our commercials once we have given them our event's details.

Hiring a street team is the main way we are going to get our event's information out there. Some quick ways that we would try to get a good street team quickly are:

- Asking the radio station if we can rent or use their street team
- Local media or marketing students
- Hiring experienced hospitality workers

We have set aside about $2,500 for our street team. As we discussed in an earlier section, we would have a meeting with our street team and develop our distribution strategy. For this event, our distribution schedule would look like this:

- First 6 weeks, distribute 10,000 concert flyers (1,650 per week for 6 weeks)
- Next 4 weeks, distribute 10,000 concert flyers (2,500 per week for 4 weeks)
- Last 2 - 3 weeks, distribute 5,000 concert flyers (1,666 - 2,500 flyers per week)
- And 10,000 after-party flyers (3,333 - 5,000 per week)

About 2 - 3 weeks prior to the event, we would have our street team start distributing the after-party flyers. We would be constantly updating our social media campaigns and other promotional materials These 2 - 3 weeks are when we want the radio station running more ads and doing ticket giveaways for the concert. Our TV ads would be running during peak times to hit our target market.

The 30 days prior to our concert will be the most important for our street team and promotional campaigns. We want as much feedback as possible from our street team and social media campaigns. This allows us to change things if necessary, answer any questions, and handle any potential issues or negative press about our concert or artists. Be creative and flexible in order to maximize ticket sales.

We are now about three days from the concert date and have pre-sold about 3,000 tickets at $40 each. That's $120,000 in gross revenue. We know we have made money, but we have to deduct our expenses. As the promoter, part of our job is to take care of the artists and their staff. We would pick them up from the airport, take them to their hotel, and make sure that they have everything they need. We would brief them on the concert schedule and when the radio station live interviews would be.

We would bring the artists to the venue for a soundcheck and then maybe dinner prior to the concert. Building rapport with the artists is important to boost our reputation and open other doors for future artists.

After the concert, the artists will typically head to their hotel to freshen up before coming to the after-party. This will give us time to prep the venue, get our cashier and door staff in place, and any other special accommodations that might be needed for the artists.

Most of your ticket sales should be online and would be deposited in our business bank account. If there were any ticket sales at the concert venue or after party venue, our cashiers would have collected the money. Before the end of the concert and the after-party, we would pay all of our cashiers, door staff, and any other event help that we may have hired. By the end of the night, EVERYONE would be paid and the remainder of the money is ours.

Now, let's calculate how much money we made with this SOLD OUT concert:

EXPENSE/ INCOME SHEET

Hip-Hop Concert

Event/Party Name: Hip-Hop Concert

Opening Date: 5/27

Budget Available: $50,000

Notes:

Expenses:

Venue:	$ 7,500
Flyers/Posters:	2,400
Street Team:	2,500
Radio:	10,000
TV:	2,500
DJ/Talent	25,500
Cashier:	400
Graphics Designer:	350
Social Media Ads:	2,500
Security Staff:	600
Wristbands:	200
Miscellaneous:	
Artists' Accommodations:	2,060
After Party Venue:	4,000

TOTAL EXPENSES: **$60,450**

Income:

Cover Charge (After Party):	$39,000
Sponsorships	11,500
Ticket Sales:	154,000
TOTAL INCOME:	**$204,500**

TOTAL INCOME:	**$204,500**
TOTAL EXPENSES:	**60,450**
TOTAL PROFIT:	**$144,050**

As you can see, this was an extremely successful event. If you build your business and do 3-4 concerts a year, you easily earn $500,000 or more annually!

We have covered a lot of material in this short book. We wanted to give you all of the best information with no B.S. Our experiences in this industry helped us grow our business and make tons of money. If you are truly passionate about building a successful business in this industry, then use the tools and advice that we have provided to you. The worksheets in this book will help you on your way, and eventually, you will learn to do some of them in your head.

Over time, your business will change and your creativity will dictate how much money you will make. Never give up! Push yourself, be honest, professional, motivated, and energetic in everything you do. Your level of success depends on how hard you are willing to push.

Use these tools, build your empire, and change your life FOREVER!

We will be posting blank versions of the worksheet templates that were used in this book on our website. We encourage you to download and use them in your business.

www.getrichpromotingpartiesandconcerts.com[1]

Please feel free to contact us if you have any questions, feedback, or success stories that you would like to share. We want to hear from you! CONTACT US AT:

getrichpromotingparties@gmail.com

---

1.   http://www.getrichpromotingpartiesandconcerts.com

www.ingramcontent.com/pod-product-compliance
Lightning Source LLC
Chambersburg PA
CBHW071118210326
41519CB00020B/6341